# CAN I HAVE A TREAT?

*This book is dedicated to Kiran and Meena*

# TABLE OF CONTENTS

Introduction..................................................................................................1

Commonly Used Ingredients.................................................................3

Strawberry Banana Popsicles................................................................5

Applesauce Muffins...................................................................................9

Chocolate Chip Ice Cream....................................................................13

Fudge Brownies........................................................................................17

Almond Butter Cups...............................................................................21

Banana Coconut Cookies.....................................................................25

Chocolate Chip Banana Bread...........................................................29

Double Chocolate Cookies..................................................................33

Chocolate Cupcakes...............................................................................37

Chocolate Frosting..................................................................................41

About The Author....................................................................................45

# INTRODUCTION

*Welcome!*

My name is Vidhya Illuri and I am an endocrinologist with an interest in culinary medicine. In addition to seeing patients with diabetes and other endocrine disorders, my other passion is creating healthy recipes in the kitchen with my two children Kiran and Meena. Every recipe in this book was designed for a child (3 years and up) to take the lead in the kitchen while the adult plays the role of sous chef. Each recipe has adult instructions as well as illustrated step by step instructions for children.

All of the recipes in this book are considered "treats." However, these are healthy treats! The recipes are all paleo-friendly and use fruit as the sweetener along with some dark chocolate. There is no added refined sugar. I hope you enjoy these recipes as much as my family does!

2

## COMMONLY USED INGREDIENTS

**Almond butter**-I use almond butter with only one ingredient-almonds! Avoid the kind with added sugar, salt, or oils

**Applesauce**-I use applesauce that has two ingredients-apples and water. Avoid the kind with added sugar

**Dark chocolate chips**-I use chocolate that is 70% cacao or above, this type of chocolate has low sugar content and has many health benefits(for the adults who are enjoying the treats as well)! Paleo dark chocolate is available at many grocery stores.

**Coconut flour**-Coconut flour is a paleo flour commonly used in baked goods-it is made with just coconut!

4

# STRAWBERRY BANANA POPSICLES
*gluten-free, vegan, paleo*

## Ingredients
*Makes 6 popsicles*

2 bananas(frozen)
1/3 cup full fat coconut milk(unsweetened)
6 strawberries with stems removed
Popsicle molds(or small disposable cups)
6 popsicle sticks

## Notes
\*\* I use frozen banana so the layers are firm enough to not mix together during the filling process

\*\* I use strawberries for the second layer, but you can use a different fruit to change the color and flavor

## Directions

1. Add frozen bananas and coconut milk to blender and blend until smooth
2. Pour half of the banana mixture into the popsicle molds filling them half-way up, reserve the other half of the banana mixture in the blender
3. Add the strawberries to the reserved banana mixture and blend until smooth
4. Layer the strawberry banana mixture into the molds on top of the banana mixture
5. Insert a popsicle stick into each mold
6. Freeze overnight
7. To remove popsicle from molds, run warm water on outside of the mold for 5-10 seconds
8. Remove popsicles and enjoy

# STRAWBERRY BANANA POPSICLES

**1.** ADD 2 FROZEN BANANAS TO BLENDER

**2.** ADD 1/3 CUP COCONUT MILK

**3.** BLEND UNTIL SMOOTH

**4.** USE HALF OF MIXTURE TO FILL MOLDS HALF FULL

**5.** ADD 6 CUT STRAWBERRIES TO REST OF MIXTURE

**6.** BLEND UNTIL SMOOTH

**7.** POUR PINK MIXTURE ON TOP OF YELLOW MIXTURE

**8.** PLACE POPSICLE STICK IN EACH MOLD

**9.** PLACE MOLDS IN FREEZER OVERNIGHT

**EAT THEM BEFORE THEY MELT!**

8

# APPLESAUCE MUFFINS
*gluten-free, paleo*

## Ingredients
*Makes 12 mini muffins*
1/2 cup almond butter(natural, unsweetened)
1/2 cup unsweetened applesauce
1 egg
1/4 teaspoon vanilla extract
1/4 teaspoon baking soda
1/8 teaspoon cinnamon
1/8 teaspoon salt

## Notes
\*\* I do not add sweetener to the recipe as the applesauce is sweet enough
\*\* It may be fun to add mix-ins such as nuts, blueberries, or dark chocolate chips!
\*\* If mix-ins are added, baking time may increase

## Directions
1. Pre-heat oven to 350 degrees Fahrenheit
2. Lightly grease a mini muffin pan with oil
3. Mix all ingredients in a bowl until combined
4. Pour batter into greased muffin pan 2/3 of the way up
5. Bake for 13-15 minutes
6. Let muffins cool in pan for 10-15 minutes
7. Remove from pan and enjoy

# APPLESAUCE MUFFINS

1. ADD 1/2 CUP ALMOND BUTTER TO BOWL
2. ADD 1/2 CUP APPLESAUCE TO BOWL
3. CRACK 1 EGG INTO BOWL
4. ADD 1/4 TEASPOON VANILLA
5. ADD 1/4 TEASPOON BAKING SODA
6. ADD 1/8 TEASPOON CINNAMON
7. ADD 1/8 TEASPOON SALT
8. MIX WELL
9. POUR BATTER INTO MINI MUFFIN PAN 2/3 OF THE WAY UP

10

**BAKE AT 350 DEGREES
FAHRENHEIT FOR 15 MINUTES**

**EAT AND ENJOY!**

12

# CHOCOLATE CHIP ICE CREAM
*gluten-free, paleo, vegan*

### Ingredients
*Makes 4 servings*
2 overripe bananas
1/4 teaspoon salt
1 teaspoon vanilla extract
3 tablespoons dark chocolate chips(70% cacao)

### Notes
** I do not add sweetener to the recipe as the bananas are sweet enough
** Depending on how powerful the blender/food processor is, bananas may need to be thawed slightly prior to blending
** If desired use paleo-friendly chocolate chips

### Directions
1. Peel and slice bananas into 1 inch pieces
2. Put bananas in freezer safe container and freeze overnight
3. Add frozen banana, salt, and vanilla to blender or food processor and blend until creamy
4. Add chocolate chips and pulse until incorporated
5. Can serve immediately for a soft serve texture
6. Can also freeze for a firmer texture

# CHOCOLATE CHIP ICE CREAM

**1** SLICE 2 BANANAS INTO 1 INCH PIECES

**2** FREEZE BANANA PIECES OVERNIGHT

**3** ADD FROZEN BANANA TO BLENDER

**4** ADD 1/4 TEASPOON SALT

**5** ADD 1 TEASPOON VANILLA

**6** BLEND UNTIL CREAMY

**7** ADD 3 TABLESPOONS CHOCOLATE CHIPS

**8** PULSE 2-3 MORE TIMES

TIME FOR A TREAT!

# FUDGE BROWNIES
*gluten-free, paleo*

## Ingredients
*Makes 8 brownies*
1 overripe banana
1 egg
1 teaspoon vanilla extract
1/4 cup unsweetened almond milk
1/4 cup cocoa powder
1/4 teaspoon baking soda
1/4 cup dark chocolate chips (70% cacao)

## Notes
\*\* I use a bread pan to make these brownies
\*\* I do not add sweetener to the recipe as the banana is sweet enough
\*\* Can use paleo-friendly chocolate chips if needed
\*\* I like to serve these warm with my chocolate chip ice cream *(see previous recipe)*

## Directions
1. Pre-heat oven to 350 degrees Fahrenheit
2. Line a bread pan with parchment paper
3. Mash banana in a large bowl until smooth
4. Add egg, vanilla, and almond milk and mix well
5. Add cocoa powder and baking soda and mix well
6. Fold in chocolate chips
7. Pour batter into lined bread pan
8. Bake for 35-40 minutes until an inserted toothpick comes out clean
9. Allow to cool in pan for 10-15 minutes
10. Cut into 8 pieces and enjoy

# FUDGE BROWNIES

1. MASH 1 BANANA IN BOWL
2. CRACK 1 EGG INTO BOWL
3. ADD 1 TEASPOON VANILLA
4. ADD 1/4 CUP ALMOND MILK
5. ADD 1/4 CUP COCOA POWDER
6. ADD 1/4 TEASPOON BAKING SODA
7. MIX WELL
8. FOLD IN 1/4 CUP CHOCOLATE CHIPS
9. POUR BATTER INTO BREAD PAN

**10**

BAKE AT 350 DEGREES FAHRENHEIT
FOR 35-40 MINUTES

EAT WHILE WARM!

20

# ALMOND BUTTER CUPS
*gluten-free, paleo, vegan*

## Ingredients
*Makes 8 almond butter cups*
1/4 cup unsweetened almond butter
2 teaspoons coconut flour
1/2 cup dark chocolate chips(70% cacao)

## Notes
** Can use paleo-friendly dark chocolate chips if needed

## Directions

1. Add almond butter and coconut flour to a bowl, mix well and set aside
2. Line mini cupcake pan with paper liners
3. Melt half of the dark chocolate chips in the microwave in 15 second intervals, stir every interval until smooth
4. Place 1/2 teaspoon of melted chocolate into each cupcake liner
5. Refrigerate cupcake pan for 15 minutes
6. Place 1 teaspoon of almond butter mixture on top of the set chocolate
7. Melt rest of chocolate chips and top each almond butter cup until almond butter is covered
8. Refrigerate for another 20 minutes
9. Unwrap and enjoy

# ALMOND BUTTER CUPS

1. ADD 1/4 CUP ALMOND BUTTER TO BOWL
2. ADD 2 TEASPOONS COCONUT FLOUR TO BOWL
3. MIX WELL
4. PUT CUPCAKE LINERS INTO MINI CUPCAKE PAN
5. POUR 1/4 CUP CHOCOLATE CHIPS IN BOWL
6. MICROWAVE CHOCOLATE UNTIL MELTED
7. POUR 1 TEASPOON CHOCOLATE INTO CUPCAKE LINER
8. REFRIGERATE FOR 15 MINUTES
9. ADD 1 TEASPOON ALMOND BUTTER MIXTURE

**10** POUR REST OF CHOCOLATE CHIPS INTO BOWL

**11** MICROWAVE CHOCOLATE UNTIL MELTED

**12** POUR SECOND LAYER OF CHOCOLATE ONTO ALMOND BUTTER

**13** REFRIGERATE FOR 20 MINUTES

TAKE A BITE!

# BANANA COCONUT COOKIES
## gluten-free, vegan, paleo

### Ingredients

*Makes 16 cookies*

2 overripe bananas
1 1/2 cup unsweetened shredded coconut
1/2 teaspoon salt
1/4 teaspoon cinnamon
1 teaspoon pure vanilla extract
3 tablespoons dark chocolate(70% cacao or higher)

### Notes

** I do not add sweetener to the recipe as the bananas are sweet enough
** I leave the food processor unplugged while the kiddos put ingredients in
** If desired, use paleo-friendly chocolate chips
** These cookies are especially good straight from the refrigerator!

### Directions

1. Pre-heat oven to 350 degrees Fahrenheit
2. Line baking sheet with parchment paper
3. Add bananas, shredded coconut, salt, cinnamon, and vanilla to a food processor
4. Blend until the batter has the consistency of pancake batter
5. Drop 1 tablespoon of batter onto the parchment lined baking sheet, approximately two inches apart
6. Bake for 20 minutes
7. Allow to cool in pan for 10 minutes
8. Remove cookies and allow to cool on wire rack
9. Melt chocolate chips in microwave safe container(microwave in 20 second intervals and stir each interval)
10. Drizzle melted chocolate over each cookie
11. Allow chocolate to set

# BANANA COCONUT COOKIES

**1.** ADD 2 BANANAS TO FOOD PROCESSOR

**2.** ADD 1 1/2 CUPS SHREDDED COCONUT

**3.** ADD 1/2 TEASPOON SALT

**4.** ADD 1/4 TEASPOON CINNAMON

**5.** ADD 1 TEASPOON VANILLA

**6.** BLEND UNTIL SMOOTH

**7.** DROP 1 TABLESPOON OF DOUGH FOR EACH COOKIE

**8.** BAKE FOR 20 MINUTES AT 350 DEGREES FAHRENHEIT

**9.** ADD 3 TABLESPOONS CHOCOLATE CHIPS

**10** MICROWAVE CHOCOLATE UNTIL MELTED

**11** DRIZZLE CHOCOLATE ONTO COOKIES

**SHARE AND EAT!**

# CHOCOLATE CHIP BANANA BREAD
*gluten-free, paleo*

## Ingredients
*Makes 12 servings*
2 overripe bananas
3 eggs
3/4 cup almond butter
1 teaspoon vanilla extract
4 tablespoons coconut flour
1 teaspoon cinnamon
1 teaspoon baking soda
1/2 teaspoon salt
3 tablespoons dark chocolate chips(70% cacao)

## Directions
1. Pre-heat oven to 350 degrees Fahrenheit
2. Grease a regular bread pan with olive oil
3. In a large mixing bowl, mash bananas with a fork until smooth
3. Add eggs, almond butter, vanilla, coconut flour, cinnamon, baking soda, and salt
4. Mix batter well with a large wooden spoon
5. Pour batter into bread pan
6. Top with dark chocolate chips
7. Bake for 30-35 minutes until an inserted toothpick comes out clean
8. Cool bread while still in pan
9. Remove loaf, slice and serve

## Notes
** I do not add sweetener to the recipe as the bananas are sweet enough
** I direct little ones to crack eggs in a separate bowl and then add them to the large bowl to avoid shells in the batter
** If desired, use paleo-friendly chocolate chips

# CHOCOLATE CHIP BANANA BREAD

**1.** MASH 2 BANANAS IN BOWL

**2.** CRACK 3 EGGS INTO BOWL

**3.** ADD 3/4 CUP ALMOND BUTTER

**4.** ADD 1 TEASPOON VANILLA EXTRACT

**5.** ADD 4 TABLESPOONS COCONUT FLOUR

**6.** ADD 1 TEASPOON CINNAMON

**7.** ADD 1 TEASPOON BAKING SODA

**8.** ADD 1/2 TEASPOON SALT

**9.** STIR WITH A LARGE SPOON

**10** POUR BATTER INTO GREASED BREAD PAN

**11** ADD 3 TABLESPOONS CHOCOLATE CHIPS

**12** BAKE AT 350 DEGREES FAHRENHEIT FOR 30-35 MINUTES

**TIME TO EAT!**

# DOUBLE CHOCOLATE COOKIES
*gluten-free, paleo*

## Ingredients

*Makes 10 cookies*
1/2 cup almond butter(natural, unsweetened)
1/2 cup unsweetened applesauce
1 egg
1/2 teaspoon vanilla extract
1/4 cup coconut flour
1/4 cup cocoa powder
1/2 teaspoon baking soda
1/4 teaspoon salt
3 tablespoons chocolate chips(70% cacao)

## Directions

1. Pre-heat oven to 350 degrees Fahrenheit
2. Line a baking sheet with parchment paper
3. Add almond butter, applesauce, egg, and vanilla to bowl and mix well
4. Add coconut flour, cocoa powder, baking soda, and salt and mix well
5. Fold in chocolate chips
6. Drop by heaping tablespoons onto baking sheet
7. Bake for 12 minutes
8. Let cool in pan for 10-15 minutes
9. Remove from pan and enjoy

## Notes

\*\* I do not add sweetener to the recipe as the applesauce is sweet enough
\*\* Can use paleo-friendly chocolate chips if needed
\*\* Can also add chopped nuts to cookie dough prior to baking

# DOUBLE CHOCOLATE COOKIES

1. ADD 1/2 CUP ALMOND BUTTER TO BOWL
2. ADD 1/2 CUP APPLESAUCE
3. CRACK 1 EGG INTO BOWL
4. ADD 1/2 TEASPOON VANILLA
5. ADD 1/4 CUP COCONUT FLOUR
6. ADD 1/4 CUP COCOA POWDER
7. ADD 1/2 TEASPOON BAKING SODA
8. ADD 1/4 TEASPOON SALT
9. MIX WELL

**10** ADD 3 TABLESPOONS CHOCOLATE CHIPS AND MIX

**11** DROP DOUGH BY HEAPING TABLESPOONS ONTO BAKING SHEET

**12** BAKE FOR 12 MINUTES AT 350 DEGREES FAHRENHEIT

# CHOCOLATE CUPCAKES
*gluten-free, paleo*

## Ingredients
*Makes 8 cupcakes*
1/2 cup unsweetened almond butter
2 eggs
1 cup applesauce
1 teaspoon vanilla extract
1/2 cup cocoa powder
1/2 teaspoon baking soda
1/2 teaspoon baking powder
Chocolate frosting(see recipe in next section)
8 raspberries

## Notes
\*\* I do not add sweetener to the recipe as the applesauce is sweet enough
\*\* See recipe for chocolate frosting in next section of this book

## Directions
1. Pre-heat oven to 350 degrees Fahrenheit
2. Line regular muffin pan with cupcake liners
3. Mix almond butter, eggs, applesauce, and vanilla in a bowl
4. Add cocoa powder, baking soda, and baking powder and mix well
5. Pour batter into lined muffin pan 2/3 of the way up
7. Bake for 25 minutes or until an inserted toothpick comes out clean
8. After cupcakes cool, top with chocolate frosting and raspberries

# CHOCOLATE CUPCAKES

**1.** PUT CUPCAKE LINERS INTO MUFFIN PAN

**2.** ADD 1/2 CUP ALMOND BUTTER TO BOWL

**3.** ADD 1 CUP APPLESAUCE TO BOWL

**4.** ADD 1 TEASPOON VANILLA TO BOWL

**5.** CRACK 2 EGGS INTO BOWL

**6.** MIX WELL

**7.** ADD 1/2 CUP COCOA POWDER

**8.** ADD 1/2 TEASPOON BAKING POWDER

**9.** ADD 1/2 TEASPOON BAKING SODA

**10** MIX WELL

**11** SPOON BATTER INTO MUFFIN PAN 2/3 OF THE WAY UP

**12** BAKE FOR 25 MINUTES AT 350 DEGREES FAHRENHEIT

**13** COOL CUPCAKES THEN TOP WITH FROSTING

**14** ADD 1 RASPBERRY TO TOP OF EACH CUPCAKE

**15** SHARE AND ENJOY!

# CHOCOLATE FROSTING
*gluten-free, paleo, vegan*

## Ingredients
*Makes 8 servings*
1 cup dark chocolate chips(70% cacao)
1/2 cup coconut milk(full fat)
1/2 teaspoon vanilla extract

## Notes
** Adults will manage the stove part of the recipe, children can manage the stirring!
** After frosting sets in the refrigerator, it may need to sit at room temperature for 10-15 minutes before spreading

## Directions
1. Heat coconut milk in sauce pan over low heat
2. After coconut milk reaches a simmer, pour over chocolate chips and add vanilla extract
3. Stir until smooth
4. Refrigerate for 2-3 hours

# CHOCOLATE FROSTING

**1.** HEAT 1/2 CUP COCONUT MILK ON STOVE

**2.** ADD 1 CUP CHOCOLATE CHIPS TO BOWL

**3.** POUR HOT COCONUT MILK OVER CHOCOLATE

**4.** ADD 1/2 TEASPOON VANILLA

**5.** STIR UNTIL SMOOTH

**6.** CHILL FOR 3 HOURS

TIME FOR A TREAT!

# ABOUT THE AUTHOR

Dr. Vidhya Illuri is a board certified endocrinologist. She completed her endocrinology and diabetes fellowship at Northwestern University in Chicago. She now lives in San Antonio with her husband, son, and daughter. Her primary interest is using healthy food to treat diabetes. She created the blog doctorspantry.org to share healthy and delicious recipes with her patients.

Made in the USA
Columbia, SC
04 January 2025